DATE DUE

Working for Planet Earth

MAURICE STRONG

by Hugh Westrup

A Gateway Green Biography
The Millbrook Press
Brookfield, Connecticut

Cover photo courtesy of Robert Semeniuk
Background cover photo courtesy of Photo Researchers

Photos courtesy of Wide World Photos: pp. 4, 43; Maurice
Strong: pp. 7, 10, 20; Bettmann: pp. 9, 19 (both); Alaska
State Library, C.L. Andrews Coll.: p. 17; The United Nations:
pp. 25, 30 (top), 35 (bottom); Davis/Greenpeace, Washington,
D.C.: p. 30 (bottom); Hevetson/Greenpeace, London: p. 35
(top); Robert Semeniuk: p. 37.

Library of Congress Cataloging-in-Publication Data
Westrup, Hugh.
Maurice Strong : working for planet Earth
by Hugh Westrup.
p.   cm. — (Gateway green biography)
Includes bibliographical references and index.
Summary: The story of the man who organized the 1992
Earth Summit as well as other programs that have been
instrumental to global environmental conservation.
ISBN 1-56294-414-2 (lib. bdg.)
1. Strong, Maurice F. — Juvenile literature.   2. Environmen-
talism — Juvenile literature.   3. United Nations Conference
on Environment and Development (1992 : Rio de Janeiro,
Brazil — Juvenile literature.   4. Environmentalists — Canada
— Biography — Juvenile literature   [1. Strong, Maurice F.
2. Environmentalists.   3. Environmental protection.]
I. Title.   II. Series.
GE56.S77W47   1994
363.7'0092 — dc20   [B]   93-41528   CIP   AC

Published by The Millbrook Press
2 Old New Milford Road
Brookfield, Connecticut 06804

Maurice Strong

Beneath a sculpture called the Tree of Life at the 1992 Earth Summit, Maurice Strong signs a pledge to protect the planet's environment for future generations.

The place was Rio de Janeiro, Brazil. The occasion was the 1992 Earth Summit, the biggest conference on the environment ever held. People from 178 nations had gathered to discuss the enormous threats facing the world's ecology. They talked about everything from saving endangered species to controlling pollution.

The summit was well under way when suddenly it was thrown into crisis. The summit's organizers wanted each country to sign an agreement on energy conservation. If countries consumed less energy, the organizers said, the atmosphere would be less polluted.

Representatives from a group of countries that export oil and gas refused to sign the agreement. They feared that their economies would suffer if the world were encouraged to conserve energy.

Maurice Strong stepped in. Strong was the chief organizer of the Earth Summit. He talked forcefully to the oil and gas exporters. He warned them that he would shut down the summit if they refused to sign the agreement. This could prove to be very embarrassing to the exporters. They could not afford to be seen as environmental villains in the eyes of the world.

Strong's tactic worked. The exporting nations signed the agreement on energy conservation. The summit resumed its course and made history in the fight against ecological destruction.

The Rio summit was a crowning achievement in the life of its chief organizer. Maurice Strong was not a world-famous figure — his was not a household name. But for twenty years he had occupied both a unique and highly influential position in the environmental movement. Time and again he had pulled together people from nations all over the world to find solutions to environmental problems, such as pollution, wildlife extinction, and overpopulation. He helped people to understand that they have only one Earth. They have to overcome their differences to preserve it. Maurice Strong showed everyone that nothing less than our future depends on it.

Maurice Frederick Strong was born on April 29, 1929, the first child of Frederick and Mary Fyfe

Mary Strong with one-year-old Maurice. Educated and well-read, Mary instilled in Maurice and all the Strong children a sense of self-confidence and determination.

Strong. (They would have three more children.) The Strong family lived in a small town on the Canadian prairies — Oak Lake, Manitoba.

Grass and farmland rolled over the hills around Oak Lake. And through the center of town ran the Canadian Pacific Railway (CPR). Frederick Strong operated the telegraph machine in the local CPR office.

The year 1929 was a landmark in modern history: It was the year the U.S. and Canadian stock markets crashed. Thousands of investors lost their money in the crash and were plunged deeply into debt. In the next few years, many businesses shrank or collapsed. Millions of people were thrown out of work. This dark era in history, which lasted for ten years, is known as the Great Depression.

The Great Depression was especially hard for the people of Canada's prairie provinces. In 1930 the worst drought in living memory hit the North American plains. Soil that had once nourished large crops dried up and blew away. The prairies became a windy "dust bowl." What little farmland survived the drought was often stripped bare by plagues of grasshoppers.

The stock market crash of 1929 devastated
many investors, like this man who was forced
to sell his car for cash. It also ruined the lives
of people who weren't investors, like the Strongs,
by causing widespread unemployment.

The Strong children pose outside their home in Oak Lake. At far left is Maurice, age 16. Despite being close, the Strong family found enduring the Great Depression very hard.

Frederick Strong was laid off from the CPR early on in the Great Depression. Unable to find a steady job, he took whatever temporary work he could find. He often labored for food and heating fuel instead of money. The Strongs lived in a series of shabby rented houses that lacked electricity, heat, and indoor plumbing. On cold winter nights, the family's clothes would freeze stiff.

Oak Lake was not always kind to families like the Strongs. To be poor in the 1930s was a shameful condition in the eyes of some people. Sons and daughters were told not to play with friends whose fathers were out of work — friends like the Strong children.

The Strongs were a close-knit family and faithful members of the United Church of Canada. Mary Strong was a brilliant woman who had graduated from college and taught school before getting married. She entertained her children by reading aloud from the works of her favorite poets, playwrights, and novelists.

Mary Strong also handed down to her children an important message: Never hold yourself back from achieving what you want in life. Other people might try to stop you, she told them, but you must always press to the limit. This message would have a powerful impact on Maurice.

Mary Strong had grown up the daughter of a doctor in a comfortable home. The hardships of raising four children in poverty weighed heavily on her spirit. A form of mental illness called depression overcame her. She fought the illness for the rest of her life and died in a mental institution at the age of fifty-six.

Despite these difficulties, Maurice was an excellent student. He skipped four grades by the time he completed school. Oak Lake's school principal, Clarence Heapy, remembered Maurice as "about the brightest boy" he had ever taught. Maurice "could read immensely and acquire a lot of knowledge in a short time."

Maurice was not just smart in school. He also showed unusual promise as a leader, though not always for a good cause. Maurice led a gang of older boys that he swore to strict discipline. Once, he ordered the gang to take the day off from school.

The next morning, Mr. Heapy demanded an explanation for the boys' absence. They could only reply: "Because Maurice told us to."

Often Maurice would play hooky by himself. He would spend the day in a large hole he had dug out of the side of a hill. This hole he called his "dungeon." From the dungeon he watched the landscape and the animals that passed by. Although he didn't know it at the time, Maurice was learning about ecology, the science of how living things relate to each other and to their surroundings. "I could never get over the wonder of a hare's turning white in the winter and brown in the summer," he said later in life. "I developed a profound respect for nature. . . . I got my larger thoughts sitting in the hills.

"Mr. Heapy would discipline me harshly for taking time off. But I would say to him, 'Look, I learned more out there.'"

Watching Maurice growing up, Mr. Heapy marveled at this boy who "was always darting here and darting there, full of creative ideas. . . . He had the urge to see everything and do everything." Sometimes the boy's restlessness worried

Mr. Heapy and his wife. They feared that Maurice would become a runaway.

Maurice would occasionally take off an entire week from school and camp out in his dungeon in the hills. Finally, at age fourteen, he dropped out of school. The year was 1943, and World War II was raging. Maurice wanted to enlist in the Army even though he was too young.

Hopping on a freight train, Maurice traveled east to the twin cities of Port Arthur and Fort William on the shore of Lake Superior. There he hid on a Great Lakes passenger ship. Once the ship set sail, Maurice came out from hiding and was put to work scrubbing the deck. He liked the job so much he decided to head for the ocean and find work on an even bigger ship. At the next port, he ran off and rode the rails back west.

Passing through Oak Lake, Maurice took the train to the end of the line, the port of Vancouver on the Pacific coast. He lied about his age and was hired as a kitchen helper on a ship transporting troops north to Alaska. One day in Vancouver, the police picked up Maurice and put him in a detention home until his father arrived. Frederick

Strong pleaded with his son to return to Oak Lake and finish high school. Maurice agreed to his father's wish.

But shortly after graduation day, Strong was off again. This time he got a job with the Hudson's Bay Company in Canada's Northwest Territories. The job took him to Chesterfield Inlet, a remote outpost near the Arctic Circle.

The Hudson's Bay Company was one of the great pioneering businesses in Canadian history. It began as a fur-trading company and grew into a chain of successful department stores. During the 1940s the company was still in the fur-trading business in Chesterfield Inlet.

The trading post's only customers in Chesterfield Inlet were Inuits. These native North Americans, who had lived in the Arctic for thousands of years, fascinated Strong. "They were very resourceful people. They didn't have wood, they didn't have metal," he said. "What struck me was how they could be so happy living in one of the harshest climates in the world."

Strong thought that his boss treated the Inuits poorly, so he left the trading post and moved in with the Inuits. He shared an igloo with an Inuit family. He hunted seals with spears.

Living with the Inuits, Strong learned their language and something even more valuable. "I learned how to listen. Living with the [Inuits], you would sit around with them and an hour would go by with no conversation. Silence is part of communication."

Strong's experience in the Canadian north was a turning point in his life. Having to survive so close to the earth deepened his connection to nature. And living with the Inuits exposed him for the first time to people whose way of life differed from his own. "[I learned to] respect people who speak a different language, who react differently to circumstances than you do. I developed a tremendous curiosity about other cultures."

In Chesterfield Inlet, Maurice Strong met Bill Richardson, a big, handsome character from Toronto, Ontario. "Wild Bill" had gone north looking for valuable kinds of rocks. Strong knew a lot about geology, a branch of science that studies the earth

*Maurice Strong lived with an Inuit family in an igloo,
like the one shown in this photo.*

through rocks. The two became fast friends. When Richardson offered him a job in Toronto, Strong accepted.

One day in Toronto, Wild Bill's wife introduced Strong to Noah Monod, a Frenchman who was an official at the newly formed United Nations. Strong was very interested in the UN. Several years earlier, he had read a newspaper article about the Atlantic Charter. This was a historic document signed during World War II by President Franklin D. Roosevelt of the United States and Prime Minister Winston Churchill of Great Britain. The charter expressed hope for a world free of war and poverty. It became one of the founding documents of the United Nations, which was established in 1946.

The idea of a world organization dedicated to ending poverty fired Strong's imagination. Having lived through the Great Depression, he believed in making the world a place where people would share more equally in their country's wealth.

With Noah Monod's help, Strong got work at the UN's headquarters, then in Queens, New York. The job required him to supply delegates with pencils, paper, and other items. In his diary

*Franklin Roosevelt
(seated, left) and
Winston Churchill
(seated, right) aboard
the British ship* H.M.S.
Prince of Wales, *on
which they signed
the Atlantic Charter.*

*A printed copy
of the charter.
The document
helped establish
the United Nations,
which played a
central role in
Strong's life.*

FIRST ANNIVERSARY OF

THE ATLANTIC CHARTER

FIRST, their countries seek no aggrandizement, territorial or other;

SECOND, they desire to see no territorial changes that do not accord with the freely expressed wishes of the peoples concerned;

THIRD, they respect the right of all peoples to choose the form of government under which they will live; and they wish to see sovereign rights and self-government restored to those who have been forcibly deprived of them;

FOURTH, they will endeavor, with due respect for their existing obligations, to further the enjoyment by all States, great or small, victor or vanquished, of access, on equal terms, to the trade and to the raw materials of the world which are needed for their economic prosperity;

FIFTH, they desire to bring about the fullest collaboration between all nations in the economic field with the object of securing, for all, improved labor standards, economic advancement and social security;

SIXTH, after the final destruction of the Nazi tyranny, they hope to see established a peace which will afford to all

nations the means of dwelling in safety within their own boundaries, and which will afford assurance that all the men in all the lands may live out their lives in freedom from fear and want;

SEVENTH, such a peace should enable all men to traverse the high seas and oceans without hindrance;

EIGHTH, they believe that all of the nations of the world, for realistic as well as spiritual reasons, must come to the abandonment of the use of force. Since no future peace can be maintained if land, sea or air armaments continue to be employed by nations which threaten, or may threaten, aggression outside of their frontiers, they believe, pending the establishment of a wider and permanent system of general security, that the disarmament of such nations is essential. They will likewise aid and encourage all other practicable measures which will lighten for peace-loving peoples the crushing burden of armaments.

Franklin D. Roosevelt
Winston S. Churchill

Maurice Strong stands before the Statue of Liberty in New York City, around the time he first began working for the United Nations.

he wrote, "I'm most impressed with the United Nations and convinced that therein lies the key to my future."

But Strong lacked the proper qualifications for a career at the UN. The doors to its higher offices were closed to anyone without a college degree. He eventually quit the UN and returned to Toronto.

Disappointed but not discouraged, Maurice Strong remembered his mother's message: Don't let anyone hold you back from achieving what you want in life. Strong decided that he would have to earn his reputation in a field that didn't require a college education. Maybe then he could find a way into the United Nations.

The path that Strong chose was unusual for a young man with his beliefs. Having grown up in a poor family during the Great Depression, he was deeply prejudiced against business. But working with Bill Richardson, he found he had a real knack for business.

He started out by promoting stocks in mining

companies. From there he climbed quickly in Canada's business world. By age thirty-five, he was president of the Power Corporation, one of the country's largest companies.

Strong was a hard worker. His mind could absorb lots of material. And he developed the leadership skills he had shown as a boy. One of his close friends said once that Strong had a boyish charm and generosity that made people extremely loyal to him. "If Maurice Strong asked me to walk barefoot up the street in the snow, I'd do it," said his friend.

During this time Strong and his young wife, Pauline (they had married in 1950), spent two years touring the world. They visited thirty countries in Europe, Asia, and Africa.

They spent all of 1953 in the East African country of Kenya. A man named Jomo Kenyatta was leading a revolutionary group called the Mau Mau in Kenya. Kenyatta and his group wanted the British rulers of Kenya to provide the people with better living conditions. Maurice Strong didn't take part in the Mau Mau rebellion. Still, he was sympathetic to the Mau Mau cause. He learned Swahili, the main language of East Africa. He would often show up at the local Young Men's Christian Association (YMCA) and talk to the people. He listened to their hopes and fears.

In 1966, Strong left the business world to become head of Canada's External Aid Office. This was a government program that gave financial aid to developing nations — nations that were just beginning to develop their natural resources and use modern technology.

Strong was well qualified for the job at External Aid. His experience with the Inuits and in Kenya had taught him how to communicate effectively with people of foreign cultures.

Maurice Strong achieved much as head of External Aid. He reorganized the office, renaming it the Canadian International Development Agency (CIDA). During his four years in office, Canadian aid to foreign countries grew from $80 million to $400 million a year.

Maurice Strong headed CIDA during an era of great prosperity for Canada. The 1960s was also a time of extraordinary change in Canada and other countries. The women's liberation movement was demanding more opportunities for women. In the United States, black Americans were marching for civil rights. And throughout the world, people were waking up to the harm being done to planet Earth.

Between the years 1900 and 1960, the number of people on Earth had almost doubled, from 1.61 to 3.02 billion. During that time, many nations around the world had entered the modern age. Factories, electricity-generating plants, cars, and other modern technology became fixtures of life in these nations. But these changes put an enormous strain on Earth's wildlife and its natural resources — its soil, air, and water. Problems arose such as smog, endangered species, dying lakes and rivers, and overpopulation.

In response to these problems, the environmental movement was born. Ordinary people began working to protect the ecology in their communities. Organizations such as Greenpeace, the World Wildlife Fund, and Pollution Probe sprouted up.

*A chemical factory in Mexico pollutes the air.
By the late 1960s, the ill effects of industry on
the environment were all too visible.*

One of the countries most sensitive to pollution was Sweden. A strange thing happened to the Swedes in the fall of 1967 when they changed their driving rules. They switched from driving on the left-hand side of the road to driving on the right side. This meant stopping traffic for a while in various parts of the country. When the cars were stopped, the air became cleaner and clearer. The Swedes were astonished.

Not long after that, two Swedish diplomats persuaded the United Nations to hold its first meeting on the environment. The UN decided to call the meeting the United Nations Conference on the Human Environment. It scheduled the conference for the spring of 1972 in Stockholm, Sweden. And the man it asked to head the conference was Maurice Strong.

Strong was an unusual choice for the job of secretary-general of the conference. He knew little about the environment. But he was a quick learner and could pull people together. And as head of CIDA, he had traveled to numerous countries and talked to many foreign leaders.

Of course, Strong was pleased when he received the job offer. His boyhood dream of working for the UN had come true. His strategy of making his mark elsewhere in the world had really worked!

The task of organizing the UN Conference on the Human Environment began on January 1, 1971. Strong was soon traveling the globe — "darting here, darting there," as his old school principal might say. He flew from one country to another, talking to presidents, prime ministers, and other powerful people. He asked scientists to prepare detailed reports on the state of the environment in each country.

For seventeen months, Strong was constantly on the go. He held meetings over breakfast. He slept on jetliners. His pockets always jingled with coins from half a dozen nations. It was an exhausting schedule, but Strong was in his element. Late night would find him still hatching new ideas for the conference. Meanwhile, his assistants would be sleeping on the office furniture. They couldn't keep up with their energetic boss.

At first, Strong had difficulty signing up countries for the conference. Many leaders knew little about the environment. As the months went by, however, Strong showed them just how serious their ecological problems were.

Strong drew upon his experience with the Inuits and people of other cultures to help him. He got on very well, for example, with Prime Minister Indira Gandhi of India. "She had this habit of sitting there for quite a while and not saying anything," Strong recalled. "It didn't bother me — I just sat back and was silent too. She liked that."

Strong's biggest challenge was convincing many of the world's developing nations to attend the conference. Their leaders wanted nothing to do with it. They feared that it would stop them from developing their natural resources and modernizing their economies. Brazil, for example, was reluctant to attend because it feared that it would be pressured to stop developing the Amazon River basin. To ease the fears of the developing countries, Strong held a series of regional meetings in Thailand, Ethiopia, Lebanon, and Mexico.

Organizing the conference gave Maurice Strong a crash course on the environment and its problems. By the time the conference opened, many were calling him an important environmentalist.

An article about him in *The New Yorker* magazine suggested that the survival of civilization depended on his efforts. Maurice Strong, it said, had been fighting "the dragon of pollution more energetically and effectively than any other person alive."

When the conference opened on June 5, 1972, 1,200 delegates from 130 nations were in attendance. Some 1,500 journalists were present too. The conference made headlines around the globe.

At the conference, Prime Minister Olaf Palme of Sweden spoke about the damage done by war to the planet. Robert McNamara, the president of the World Bank, said that poverty was the world's number one pollutant: Many poor countries can't even provide clean living conditions for their people. Every year, millions of children die from diarrhea caused by polluted water and poor sanitation.

Strong himself gave a major speech at the opening session of the conference. He talked about environmental issues that would occupy the world's attention for the next twenty years. He spoke of polluted oceans, the destruction of forests, and the loss of animal life.

CHAIRMAN

*Strong used his
communication
skills throughout
the conference.
Here he leaps to
answer a chal-
lenging question
on the environment.*

*An area of Brazilian
rain forest being
cleared by fire. In
his speech at the
conference, Strong
pointed out how
actions taken in one
part of the environ-
ment affect all parts:
Smoke from deforest-
ation fires pollutes
the air, and the re-
duced number of
trees disrupts many
animals' way of life.*

Strong also talked about global warming. Many scientists worry about a buildup in the atmosphere of gases such as carbon dioxide, methane, and nitrous oxide. These gases are released into the air when forests and fossil fuels (oil and gasoline) are burned. Scientists think that a buildup of these gases may be trapping more and more of the sun's heat energy in the earth's atmosphere. The gases let sunlight reach the earth but keep the earth's heat from escaping. The effect is similar to what takes place in a greenhouse. That is why this process is known as the greenhouse effect. The greenhouse effect could make the atmosphere warmer in the years ahead. Ice caps at the world's poles could melt and this could raise sea levels. As a result, huge floods could follow.

In his speech, Strong also stressed the central point of the conference. Environmental destruction, he said, is a global problem. It can be tackled only through cooperation between the nations of the world.

"The wastes that pour from our homes and factories poison the water supplies and endanger the health of our neighbors. In some cases by solving our own local environmental problems, we help solve the larger international problems," he said.

Strong did not expect the conference to bring about any quick fixes. Pollution wouldn't instantly disappear from the face of the earth. Over the long term, however, the conference made an enormous impact. It awoke many nations to the problem of ecological destruction. Hundreds of new laws were soon passed in these countries to protect the environment.

The conference's other main achievement was the creation of a new UN organization, the United Nations Environment Program (UNEP). The UNEP's offices were built in Nairobi, the capital of Kenya. And the person chosen to head the program was Maurice Strong.

The UNEP opened in a splendid ceremony on October 2, 1973. To a fanfare of trumpets, the UN flag was raised to the top of a tall pole. Forest rangers and game wardens marched by. Then, as the trumpets died, the president of Kenya (and former revolutionary) Jomo Kenyatta stepped up to the platform and shouted *"Harambee."* The crowd jumped up and replied *"Harambee."* Several times

Kenyatta repeated the shout, and each time the crowd echoed him.

Harambee is a Swahili word that means "Let's pull together." It was a familiar word to every Kenyan. It also captured the spirit of the new program. Under the direction of Maurice Strong, the UNEP would be "pulling together" countries from around the world in the fight against pollution.

Strong undertook the UNEP job with his usual enthusiasm. He oversaw many projects, including Earthwatch. This was a series of monitoring stations that watched the oceans, the atmosphere, and the forests. The stations would alert governments to environmental problems needing attention.

Strong also worked on projects that involved other UN agencies and the scientific community. These projects tackled pollution in the Mediterranean Sea, health problems caused by pollution, and environmental education.

The UNEP also helped enforce the Ocean Dumping Convention. This was an agreement signed by the world's seagoing nations. It called for an end to dumping hazardous wastes and toxic chemicals into the oceans.

After four years as head of the UNEP, Strong resigned and returned to Canada. There he joined the government of Prime Minister Pierre Elliott Trudeau. His first assignment was to set up a government-owned oil company, Petro-Canada. From there he moved to other jobs.

In 1985 the United Nations came calling again. Central Africa was in crisis. War and famine were threatening the lives of some 30 million Africans. The UN wanted Strong to organize emergency relief efforts.

Strong helped raise $4 billion in food, medical supplies, and materials. He also managed the difficult task of getting the food and supplies through to those who desperately needed them. Central Africa was in chaos, and Strong had to confront some extremely hostile leaders.

Strong had experienced many hardships during his childhood. But the suffering in Africa was like nothing he had ever seen during the Great Depression. The people were so underfed they looked like living skeletons. In the end, one million

A ship dumps toxic waste at sea in this photo. One of Strong's major accomplishments with the UNEP was stopping ocean dumping, which poses hazards to human and marine environments.

A victim of the famine that devastated Africa during the mid-1980s. Strong headed the UN's program to feed the starving. The misery he saw during that time affected him deeply.

Africans perished in the famine. But millions more would have died without UN relief.

The famine in Africa was caused by many things — poverty, drought, political upheaval. It was also the result of an environmental catastrophe. The Africans couldn't feed themselves because they had put too much stress on the land and destroyed it. The soil in large areas of Africa is very fragile. It needs trees to constantly renew it. Leaves from trees fall to the ground, decay, and enrich the soil. But the Africans had cut down large expanses of forest for firewood. The soil had turned into a hard crust that couldn't be used for growing crops. Strong encouraged African governments to stop cutting trees.

When Strong finished his famine relief work he returned to North America for a rest. He and his second wife, Hanne Marstrand, owned a large piece of land in a valley in southern Colorado. There they built a home and formed the Manitou Foundation, an organization that gives parcels of land to traditional religious groups. The foundation also runs an organic farm and helps sponsor summer environmental camps that train young people to restore the planet.

Strong strolls through the Colorado valley where
he and his wife set up the Manitou Foundation.
Among its many projects, the foundation trained
young people to work on the environment's behalf.

At this point, Maurice Strong could look back with pride on his life. He was father to five children, including a foster child from Hungary. He had become a multimillionaire. He had occupied important posts in government. He had realized his dream of working for the United Nations. Through it all, he had remained a modest, approachable man. He had always shunned displays of wealth. He preferred living in humble homes. He usually drove his own car or rode in taxis instead of chauffeur-driven limousines.

The most important chapter in Maurice Strong's life, however, was just beginning. The time was December 1986. Strong was having lunch with the prime minister of Sweden, Ingvar Carlsson. The two talked about the Stockholm conference in 1972. Then Strong suggested that the United Nations mark the conference's twentieth anniversary by having a second conference on environmental issues. Prime Minister Carlsson liked the idea and took it back to the UN.

The UN saw an urgent need for such a conference. There were 1.7 billion more people living on Earth than in 1972. The number of polluting factories, power plants, and cars had increased tremendously too.

Concern for the environment had also reached an all-time high. In 1986 a huge explosion rocked the Chernobyl nuclear reactor in what was then the Soviet Union. The blast released a cloud of deadly radiation into the atmosphere, poisoning many people.

"The Stockholm conference had alerted the world to the problem of environmental destruction," said Strong. "But, on the whole, the condition of the planet was worse."

The UN decided that the second conference would be a "summit." Representatives from 178 countries would attend, and so would their leaders. Rio de Janeiro, Brazil, was picked as the site of the summit. And the person chosen to head the summit was, once again, Maurice Strong.

To organize the conference, Maurice Strong returned to his old role of global traveling salesman. Hopping from one country to the next, he practically lived on airlines. He sometimes stayed up all night talking with world leaders. Strong's spirit was as buoyant as ever even though he was sixty years old and living with diabetes. He depended on a daily insulin shot.

In preparing for the conference, Strong felt there was an absence of leadership in the world on ecological issues. The United States had once been the leading nation in environmental affairs. But it could no longer be counted on. Its president, George Bush, was doubtful about the conference. He feared that it would harm the interests of businesses in the United States.

In the absence of leadership from the United States, Strong devised a plan. He decided to get ordinary people interested in the summit.

By the late 1980s the average passenger on Spaceship Earth was better informed about the environment than ever before. Concerned citizens were setting up recycling programs in their towns and cities. Their children were doing the same thing at school. Environmental groups had sprung up throughout the world. In 1990 the twentieth anniversary of Earth Day was celebrated by 200 million people in 140 countries.

As Strong reached out to concerned citizens, he also persuaded newspaper and TV journalists to report on the upcoming conference. He hoped that all the publicity and public concern would convince politicians that they had to go to the summit.

His strategy worked. The Earth Summit turned out to be the biggest gathering of world leaders in history. Ten thousand delegates attended it. Twice as many journalists were there than had ever attended any other summit. The eyes and ears of the world were on Rio.

The conference opened on June 3, 1992. Representatives immediately began discussing a wide range of environmental issues. Often the discussions grew into arguments. Sometimes the arguments became so heated that the conference seemed about to collapse. For example, the Vatican — the seat of the Roman Catholic Church — objected to an agreement on population control because it involved birth control.

Into the midst of this and other conflicts stepped Maurice Strong. Experience had taught him that conferences always lurch from crisis to crisis. Strong knew that he had to be calm yet tough when dealing with politicians. With the skills of a master negotiator, he settled the disputes. The conference sailed through to a hopeful finish.

In the end, most of the delegates signed two important treaties. The first concerned *global warming*. The agreement aimed to control the production of greenhouse gases, such as methane and carbon dioxide.

Delegates also signed a treaty to protect the planet's *biodiversity* — its broad range of plant and animal species. The treaty called for stopping the destruction of many wildlife habitats around the planet. When these habitats disappear, many wildlife species do too.

The summit's third major accomplishment was the creation of a new UN commission on *sustainable development*. This was a new idea in the environmental movement. It recognized that economic growth is essential to reduce poverty. Growth brings better jobs and improved living conditions. At the same time, growth depends on preserving air, water, and other ecological resources. Human activity must be balanced with nature's ability to renew itself.

*Children played an active role throughout the
1992 Earth Summit. Here children write messages to
world leaders on a giant flag. The messages ask them
to protect the environment for future generations.*

None of these accomplishments would have been possible without Maurice Strong. Strong has not been a typical environmentalist. He hasn't made scientific discoveries like those made by Jane Goodall while observing the chimps in Africa. He hasn't started any organizations like Friends of the Earth. The idea of sustainable development isn't even his.

But his role has been no less important. Before ideas like sustainable development can change the world, they must be brought to its attention. And that is what Maurice Strong has done. He has pulled world leaders together to confront some of Earth's most pressing problems. More than that, he has introduced the leaders to ideas that will help solve these problems. In these ways, he has been a tireless worker for planet Earth.

Important Dates

April 29, 1929	Maurice Frederick Strong is born in Oak Lake, Manitoba, Canada.
1943	Leaves home for the first time and finds work on a ship transporting troops to Alaska.
1945	Lives with Inuits in northern Canada.
1947	Moves to New York City to work at the United Nations.
1953	Spends a year with his first wife in Africa.
1964	Works for the Power Corporation.
1966	Appointed head of Canada's External Aid Office.
June 1972	United Nations Conference on the Human Environment takes place in Stockholm, Sweden.
October 1973	United Nations Environment Program opens its offices in Nairobi, Kenya.
1985	Leads famine relief efforts in Africa.
June 1992	Earth Summit takes place in Rio de Janeiro, Brazil.

Find Out More

About the Environment

Caring for Our Forests by Carol Greene. Hillside, N.J.: Enslow, 1991.

The Environmental Detective Kit by Douglas Herridge and Susan Hughes. New York: HarperCollins, 1991.

The Greenhouse Effect by Michael Bright. New York: Franklin Watts, 1991.

Rads, Ergs and Cheeseburgers: The Kid's Guide to Energy and the Environment by Bill Yanda. Santa Fe, N.M.: John Muir, 1991.

About the United Nations

The Story of the United Nations by Conrad R. Stein. Chicago: Childrens Press, 1986.

The United Nations by Carol Greene. Chicago: Childrens Press, 1983.

Index